SPORTS
ALL-ST★RS

SERENA WILLIAMS

Elliott Smith

Lerner Publications ◆ Minneapolis

To Ava and Xavier—keep serving aces!

Copyright © 2021 by Lerner Publishing Group, Inc.

All rights reserved. International copyright secured. No part of this book may be reproduced, stored in a retrieval system, or transmitted in any form or by any means—electronic, mechanical, photocopying, recording, or otherwise—without the prior written permission of Lerner Publishing Group, Inc., except for the inclusion of brief quotations in an acknowledged review.

Lerner Publications Company
An imprint of Lerner Publishing Group, Inc.
241 First Avenue North
Minneapolis, MN 55401 USA

For reading levels and more information, look up this title at www.lernerbooks.com.

Main body text set in Albany Std 22. Typeface provided by Agfa.

Editor: Shee Yang **Designer:** Mary Ross

Library of Congress Cataloging-in-Publication Data

Names: Smith, Elliott, 1976– author. | Lerner Publications Company. | Lerner Publishing Group, Inc.
Title: Serena Williams / Elliott Smith.
Description: Minneapolis : Lerner Publications, 2021. | Series: Sports All-Stars (Lerner Sports) | Includes bibliographical references and index. | Audience: Ages 7–11 years | Audience: Grades 2–3 | Summary: "Known as one of America's greatest athletes of all time, Serena Williams has shattered ceilings and empowered people all around the world. Check out this title about tennis living legend Serena Williams!"— Provided by publisher.
Identifiers: LCCN 2020003641 (print) | LCCN 2020003642 (ebook) | ISBN 9781728414737 (Library Binding) | ISBN 9781728414959 (Paperback) | ISBN 9781728414966 (eBook)
Subjects: LCSH: Williams, Serena, 1981–—Juvenile literature. | African American women tennis players— Biography—Juvenile literature. | Women tennis players—United States—Biography—Juvenile literature. | U.S. Open (Tennis tournament)—History—Juvenile literature. | Wimbledon Championships—History—Juvenile literature. | Internationaux de France de tennis, Roland Garros—History—Juvenile literature. | Tennis—History— Juvenile literature. | Racism in sports. | Women philanthropists—Biography—Juvenile literature.
Classification: LCC GV994.W55 S65 2021 (print) | LCC GV994.W55 (ebook) | DDC 796.342092 [B]—dc23

LC record available at https://lccn.loc.gov/2020003641
LC ebook record available at https://lccn.loc.gov/2020003642

Manufactured in the United States of America
1-48654-49077-4/8/2020

CONTENTS

HISTORY MAKER

Serena Williams prepares to send the tennis ball to Venus Williams during day 13 of the Australian Open.

Serena Williams looked across the net at a familiar face during the final match of the 2017 Australian Open singles. Her opponent was her older sister, Venus Williams. With history on the line, there was no other player she would rather face.

FACTS AT A GLANCE

- **Date of birth:** September 26, 1981

- **Position:** singles and doubles tennis player

- **League:** Women's Tennis Association (WTA)

- **Professional highlights:** won 73 titles and 23 **Grand Slam** titles; ranked first eight times for women's tennis; highest-earning tennis player of all time from tournaments

- **Personal highlights:** has one daughter; is a successful fashion designer; is a part owner of the Miami Dolphins; works as a UNICEF Goodwill Ambassador; started the Serena Williams Fund

The Williams sisters share an embrace after competing against each other in the 2017 Australian Open.

As they had done many times before, the Williams sisters battled each other hard. Serena Williams delivered her powerful **serves**. *Thwack!* Venus Williams answered with sharp **strokes**. *Crack!* The tension of the match hung in the air. After almost 90 minutes, Serena Williams claimed a 6–4, 6–4 win. She let herself fall to the ground in joy.

The emotional victory gave Williams 23 singles wins in Grand Slam tennis tournaments—the most by any man or woman since 1968. It made official what most fans already knew: Williams was the best women's tennis player in history. And even though she had beaten her sister, Serena Williams was happy to share the moment with her.

"I felt like it was more just a celebration for everything we've done in sports, everything we've done for women, everything we've tried to do to inspire people," Williams said. "My first big match against Venus was right here on this stadium court. I felt like everything had really come full circle."

Making her triumph more impressive was something that was revealed later. She was eight weeks pregnant during the Australian Open. She didn't lose a set the entire tournament.

Venus Williams returns a shot to Serena Williams during the final match of the 2017 Australian Open.

BREAKING
BARRIERS

Serena (right) and Venus pose with their father at tennis camp.

From an early age, Serena was a tennis prodigy. It was the rest of the tennis world that needed to catch up.

Serena with her father, Richard

Serena started playing tennis in Compton, California, at the age of four alongside her sister. Their father, Richard Williams, didn't know much about tennis. But he created a plan that he thought would help his daughters grow their talents. His plan worked. The family moved to Florida when Serena was nine so she and Venus could practice year-round and attend a tennis academy. They were already prepared for more serious training.

But their father pulled Serena and Venus out of youth tournaments because of **racism**. Many tennis players come from wealthy white families. Serena and Venus didn't fit into either of those categories. It was the start of a long and ongoing fight against racism for Serena.

In 1995, a 14-year-old Serena made her professional debut. At 16, she made her Grand Slam debut at the Australian Open, where she lost to Venus in the second round.

Serena lunges forward to return the ball during the 1998 French Open in Paris.

Serena and Venus Williams have played against each other 30 times professionally. Serena Williams holds an 18—12 lead, including a 7—2 edge in Grand Slam finals.

From there, Serena Williams's career took off. She won her first pro singles title at the age of 18 in 1999. Later that year, she earned her first US Open victory. She became the second African American woman to win a Grand Slam singles title in 43 years. The first was Althea Gibson.

Her achievements continued to grow. In 2002, at 20 years old, she rose to first place in the tennis ranking system. Williams also won the last three majors of that year: Wimbledon, the French Open, and the US Open. When she won the 2003 Australian Open, Williams became only the fifth woman to hold all four titles at the same time. This became known as the Serena Slam.

Williams has had unbelievable success since her early days. She was ranked first for 186 weeks straight. She has won more than 830 matches. And she overcame serious injuries on several occasions. But her proudest accomplishment is becoming a role model.

"When I first started, there weren't a lot of people who looked like me," Williams said. "So it was really important to always help other people feel as if this is something they could also be a part of."

Serena prepares to return opponent Pavlina Stoyanova-Nola's shot during the 1998 US Open.

Williams at practice before the 2008 Australian Open

The best athletes never rest on their success. For Williams, this means playing tennis nearly every day. Practice makes perfect, and Williams takes her practice seriously.

Williams works on her backhand during a practice session before the 2017 Australian Open.

Williams warming up in Melbourne before the start of the 2017 Australian Open

Williams spends about four hours on the court with her coach daily. During that time, she hits hundreds of tennis balls. She practices serving the ball with her **forehand** and her **backhand**.

Williams is one of the best servers in tennis. She once blasted a serve at around 128 miles (206 km) per hour during the Australian Open. It remains the fifth-fastest serve by a woman ever. She spends time on every element of her serve to get it right. While practicing, Williams bounces the ball five times before tossing it on her first serve. On her second serve, she only bounces the ball twice. She spends 10 minutes tossing the ball in the air. Williams wants the ball to go straight up without any spin on it.

Williams bends to take a careful look at her shot during the Eastbourne Aegon International in Britain on June 11, 2011.

Another mark of a great player is being able to get to the opponents' shots. According to tennis studies, the average distance run during a tennis match is 3 miles (4.8 km). For Williams to keep winning, she must stay in shape.

Williams does a mix of running, biking, and strength training. With a trainer, she completes a variety of exercises designed to help with endurance and flexibility. In one of them, Williams runs across a **baseline** to start. She then makes quick stops and starts while shuffling her feet. This helps her build a fast reaction time.

Williams also watches her diet. During the tennis season, she eats mostly plant-based foods. But occasionally, she eats fish and chicken.

One surprising element Williams adds to her workout is dance. It's a good fit for her fun-loving personality. "I dance a lot when I'm healthy," Williams said. "It's a fun way to get a workout in instead of going to the gym and jumping on the treadmill for 30 minutes. I really enjoy that."

Williams dances in celebration after earning her gold medal match at the 2012 Olympic Games in London.

Williams has shined on the court for the United States. As of 2020, she had won four women's tennis Olympic gold medals.

Williams and her daughter, Olympia, pose alongside her first-place trophy at the Auckland Classic on January 12, 2020.

Tennis has always been a huge part of Williams's life. But it's not the only part. She also loves spending time with her husband and daughter.

Williams's husband, Alexis Ohanian, with their daughter, Olympia

Williams gave birth to her daughter, Olympia, in September 2017. She and her husband, Alexis Ohanian, cofounder of Reddit, are enjoying parenthood. Williams brings Olympia to all of her tennis tournaments and likes sharing funny pictures of her on social media. "Being around her every day is super important, and I want her to have just a great upbringing, the best way that I know how," Williams said.

Williams is a pet lover as well. Her teacup Yorkshire terrier, Chip, and Shih Tzu, Lauralei, travel with Williams and have also appeared in many of her social media posts.

Williams enjoys staying busy with her many passions outside of tennis. Known for wearing unique outfits during tournaments, she is heavily involved in fashion. Williams has created jewelry, handbags, and clothing lines. Her newest line, S by Serena, offers clothing for women featuring a stylish S logo.

Williams is an adviser for several businesses. In 2014, she created an investment company, Serena Ventures.

Williams and Chip out for a run

Williams (center) attends Tennis in the City on April 7, 2003, in Charleston, South Carolina.

The company invests money in smaller companies that embrace **diversity**. She and her sister, Venus Williams, made history when they became part owners of the Miami Dolphins. They are the first African American women to have an ownership stake in an American professional football team.

Williams has appeared in a number of commercials. She made appearances in the movies *Pixels* and *Ocean's 8*. And her voice was used in the cartoons *The Simpsons* and *The Legend of Korra*.

Williams (*left*) and her sister (*right*) pose with Mayor Aja Brown at the Healthy Compton 2016 Community Festival on November 12, 2016, in Compton, California.

Williams also likes to give back. Her organization, the Serena Williams Fund, helps build schools in places such as Kenya and Jamaica. She works with Venus Williams on other community projects too. The sisters helped refurbish tennis courts and opened a community center in Compton, California.

make her dream happen. As a child, she would cut socks to make clothes for her dolls. Later, she studied fashion while balancing her tennis career.

Williams designs clothes for her fashion line. And since she's the boss, she can get creative and make whatever she likes!

"My biggest joy is that I know that I'm doing something that I've always wanted to do, that I always dreamed of doing," Williams said.

Williams greets the audience on the runway with her daughter after her S by Serena Williams spring 2020 release show during New York Fashion Week.

THE G.O.A.T.

Serena prepares for a serve during the 2020 Australian Open.

Even as she enters the end of her tennis career, Williams still wants to be number one in the WTA again. While many players her age are retiring, she continues to do well. Williams made the finals at both the Wimbledon Open

Margaret Court during her Wimbledon semifinal match on July 1, 1970

and the US Open in 2018 and 2019. She wants to surpass Margaret Court's 24 Grand Slam singles titles.

Williams won her first title in almost three years in early 2020. The win was special because it was the first one she shared with her daughter. "I feel so fortunate and blessed to just be out here and be healthy and to play," Williams said. "I've been out here for so long and been through so much. It's good to be able to come and do what I do. I feel so happy to do something that I absolutely love."

Williams with her women's singles title trophy at the 2015 Wimbledon Championship

In late 2019, the Associated Press named Williams its Female Athlete of the Decade. The award noted that she won 37 singles titles during the previous 10 years. That was 11 more than any other player. She also reached the finals in at least one Grand Slam every year since her professional career began.

Williams isn't thinking about retirement yet. She's still having fun playing tennis.

Williams holds up her trophy after coming in first for women's singles at the 2015 French Open.

Her competitive nature is still kicking in. "I've been playing tennis since before my memories started," she said. "At my age, I see the finish line. And when you see the finish line, you don't slow down. You speed up."

That's why Williams will be remembered as a G.O.A.T.—one of the greatest athletes of all time.

All-Star Stats

Williams won a second Grand Slam in 2015, making her the oldest singles player to reach number one in the WTA rankings, and then she went on to win a third Grand Slam that year. She doesn't hold the record for the most Grand Slam singles titles. Margaret Court, with 24, holds the all-time record, though Williams won all of her titles in the more competitive **Open Era**, when both professionals and amateurs could enter Grand Slams.

Player	Grand Slam Singles Titles
Margaret Court	24
Serena Williams	23
Steffi Graf	22
Helen Wills Moody	19
Chris Evert	18
Martina Navratilova	18
Billie Jean King	12

Glossary

backhand: a stroke with the back of the hand turned in the direction in which the hand is moving

baseline: the line indicating the back of the court

diversity: a range of different things or people

forehand: a stroke with the palm of the hand turned in the direction in which the hand is moving

Grand Slam: the four most important tennis tournaments, consisting of the Australian Open, Wimbledon, the French Open, and the US Open

Open Era: the current era of professional tennis, when both professionals and amateurs can enter Grand Slams

prodigy: a gifted child

racism: bad or abusive behavior toward members of a different race

serves: throwing balls into the air and hitting them over a net to start playing tennis

strokes: hitting balls with a tennis racket

Source Notes

7 Johnette Howard, "GOAT Debate Over: Serena Williams and Everyone Else," ESPN, January 28, 2017, https://www.espn.com/espnw/sports/story/_/id/18571644/australian-open-goat-debate-serena-williams-everyone-else.

12 Cori Murray, "The Future of Serena Williams: The Tennis Superstar and Designer Is Ready to Conquer More," *Essence*, August 8, 2019, https://www.essence.com/feature/serena-williams-essence-magazine-cover-story-september-2019/.

17 Julia Mazziotta, "Serena Williams Loves Dancing as a Workout during Her Off-Season: 'I Really Enjoy That,'" *People*, November 21, 2016, https://people.com/bodies/serena-williams-loves-dancing-workout-off-season/.

19 Stephanie Ruhle, "Serena Williams Opens Up about Balancing Tennis and 'Mom Guilt,'" NBC, August 30, 2018, https://www.nbcnews.com/better/pop-culture/serena-williams-opens-about-balancing-career-mom-guilt-ncna904886.

23 Howard, "Serena Williams."

25 Alex Butler, "Serena Williams Ends Tennis Title Drought in New Zealand," UPI, January 13, 2020, https://www.upi.com/Sports_News/2020/01/13/Serena-Williams-ends-tennis-title-drought-in-New-Zealand/5101578915757/.

27 Rob Haskell, "Serena Williams on Motherhood, Marriage, and Making Her Comeback," *Vogue*, January 10, 2018, https://www.vogue.com/article/serena-williams-vogue-cover-interview-february-2018.

Fishman, Jon M. *Serena Williams*. Minneapolis: Lerner Publications, 2017.

Monnig, Alex. *Serena Williams*. Minneapolis: SportsZone, 2018.

Serena Williams: Women's Tennis Association
https://www.wtatennis.com/players/230234/serena-williams

Shepherd, Jodie. *Serena Williams: A Champion on and off the Court*. New York: Children's Press, 2017.

Tennis Facts for Kids
https://kids.kiddle.co/Tennis

Wetzel, Dan. *Serena Williams*. New York: Henry Holt, 2019.

Index

Photo Acknowledgments

Image credits: GREG WOOD/AFP/Getty Images, pp. 4-5; Scott Barbour/Getty Images, p. 6; Clive Brunskill/Getty Images, p. 7; Ken Levine/Allsport/Getty Images, p. 8; Rick Maiman/Sygma/Getty Images, p. 9; Clive Brunskill/Allsport/Getty Images, p. 10; CAROL NEWSOM/AFP/Getty Images, p. 12; PAUL CROCK/AFP via Getty Images, pp. 13, 14; Photo by Ryan Pierse/Getty Images, p. 15; Bryn Lennon/Getty Images, p. 16; LUIS ACOSTA/AFP/Getty Images, p. 17; Hannah Peters/Getty Images, p. 18; TONY ASHBY/AFP/Getty Images, p. 19; PETER WIDING/SCANPIX SWEDEN/ AFP/Getty Images, p. 20; Matthew Stockman/Getty Images, p. 21; Jerritt Clark/ Getty Images, p. 22; Victor VIRGILE/Gamma-Raph/Getty Images, p. 23; Jonathan DiMaggio/Getty Images, p. 24; Pictorial Parade/Getty Images, p. 25; Cynthia Lum/ Icon Sportswire/Corbis/Icon Sportswire/Getty Images, p. 26; Jon Buckle/EMPICSPA Images/Getty Images, p. 27.

Cover: Clive Brunskill/Getty Images.